A Badger Book

Men of the Sea

by
Willa Morley

Illustrated by
Robert Pious

WHITMAN PUBLISHING COMPANY
Racine, Wisconsin

Contents

KURT CARLSEN

The Enemy Sea

In the icy winter waters of the North Atlantic, a battered, broken ship was fighting for her life. Sixty-foot waves, as tall as a five-story house, pounded at her. Wild hurricane winds tossed her about like a rubber ball. Her name was the *Flying Enterprise*. And, after days of battling the stormy seas, she now lay almost on her side.

Vessels which had answered her distress call stood by. Their crews stared at the great ship, now dark and silent in the starless night. But they were not watching the ship itself. All eyes were fixed on a lone figure clinging to her bridge!

The man on the bridge was the only person left aboard the *Flying Enterprise*. He was her skipper, Captain Kurt Carlsen. And he meant to stay with her as long as she was afloat, whether she lay on her keel—*or* her side! What's more, he meant to *save* the *Flying Enterprise!* He was sure that he could take her safely home!

9

This young captain, whose story was to shake the whole world, was born in Denmark on February 14, 1914. At fourteen he joined the Danish Merchant Marine as a cook and deck boy. Ten years later he came to America and soon after that became a skipper for the Isbrandtsen Shipping Company. Now, in 1951, he had been master of their cargo ship, the *Flying Enterprise,* and an American citizen, for over three years.

Since December 22, the day they had left Hamburg, Germany, this trip had been a bad one. Almost every vessel in "winter North Atlantic" was having trouble in the worst weather many seamen had ever seen.

When only a few days out, there was a terrible roar—the hull of the *Flying Enterprise* had split across the Number Three hatch! Captain Carlsen knew that if the storms continued, his ship would crack even wider apart. Already she was beginning to list as sea water poured into her hold. As if this weren't enough, the steering oar suddenly broke away! Helpless and out of control, the stricken ship swung broadside to the waves. Again and again she took the smashing blows of the gigantic whitecaps.

The S O S went out! Rescue ships hurried to her aid. Captain Carlsen ordered his ten passengers and forty-man crew to abandon ship at once! They were taken aboard the rescue vessels.

Now the captain was alone on his deserted ship. The *Flying Enterprise* lay on her side at a fifty-degree list—some said it was sixty-five. Her skipper had to walk on his hands and feet, monkey-style, along the sloping decks. The ship was in total darkness; the power had gone. Only the captain's flashlight lighted his dangerous way. A small battery-powered radio was his only contact with the nearby ships.

It was a topsy-turvy world in which Captain Carlsen now lived. He chose the wireless room for his cabin. Here the floor was a wall, and a wall had become the floor. The bunk slanted so much the captain slid right out of it! And so he made a bed of pads and blankets in the V between the *back* of a couch and part of the *wall*. Here, at least, he could take short naps. But the icy winds and spray blowing into the open door of his cabin kept him freezing wet. The door *must* stay open in case he needed to escape. He did not know at what moment his ship might go down!

For six days and nights Captain Carlsen stayed alone on his crippled ship. Her cargo of pig iron had shifted, then settled. She seemed ready to lie there forever like a great, lazy whale. But she was still afloat! Her skipper was surer than ever that she could be towed safely home!

On January 4 the *Turmoil* finally came alongside. This sturdy little boat was one of the most powerful tugs in the world. Her crew tried to throw a towline over to the captain. He tried to grab it with one hand while holding on for dear life to the railing with the other. The choppy sea made it impossible.

The *Turmoil's* crew, soaked from waves breaking over their decks, anxiously watched as their own Captain Parker maneuvered in, dangerously close. A huge wave suddenly smacked the stern of the tug and *threw* her against the *Flying Enterprise!*

As the ships hit, the *Turmoil's* young mate, Kenneth Dancy, grabbed the stern rail of the *Flying Enterprise*. The tug slid away—and Dancy was left dangling from the rail over the boiling sea, without a life jacket. As he saw the towline flash past his head, he caught it. He climbed over the rail and handed the line to Captain Carlsen!

Together the two men pulled in the heavy line and secured it.

"Congratulations, Captain Carlsen," said Dancy as they shook hands.

"Welcome to the *Flying Enterprise,*" said the dauntless skipper with a grin.

Now that the *Turmoil* had pulled away, the captain was no longer alone. He had a passenger who was also a mate!

Dancy was to spend six days aboard, before the *Flying Enterprise* came to the end of her voyage. He made a rough bed like the captain's in the V between the sloping *floor* and the *bottom* of the couch. And now he shared the skipper's meals of fruitcake, the only thing left to eat on board!

For the next few days the tow went well. They were moving at three, then three and a half knots toward the port of Falmouth, England. Around the world people everywhere were following the day-by-day news stories of the journey of the crippled ship and her brave captain.

But suddenly the wind and sea again turned rough. Another storm was on its way! With less than sixty miles to port, the gale hit full blast! The towline snapped—and the *Flying Enterprise* was once more adrift in an angry sea.

The storm held through the following day. The valiant ship was now even *lower* in the water! She was losing her battle with the elements.

Captain Carlsen and Mate Dancy retreated from the icy wind and spray into their topsy-turvy cabin. They watched the seas creep higher and higher. The time was short.

And then the sea suddenly crashed into their little room! They must abandon ship at once!

Quickly the two men looked for the safest jump-off spot. It would have to be from the funnel! Slipping, falling, half-crawling, the captain and his mate inched along the great smokestack to its top, now its *end* as it lay out over the water. Dancy jumped—and disappeared under a huge wave! Captain Carlsen, the last man to leave his ship, quickly followed Dancy. Joining hands in the freezing water, the two men looked back at the lost ship, then swam for the *Turmoil*.

Shivering with cold and weariness, the men were hoisted aboard the tug. The crew wrapped them in warm blankets.

A second later they heard a shout.

"She's going now!" Captain Parker called.

Dancy, too tired to move, stayed in his bunk. But Captain Carlsen, out on deck, grimly watched his brave ship go down. She had fought a valiant battle. And she might have won it had the sea not been so determined to claim her.

The captain returned home to find himself a world-wide hero. But he wanted none of the fame and riches offered him. His answer was that he was a *shipmaster*—and he had only been doing his *job* in trying to save his ship!

The only reward he wanted was another ship to captain. His company gave it to him. And to honor his heroic deed, they named it the *Flying Enterprise II*.

JAMES COOK

Inside the Reef

On April 19, 1770 at 6 a.m., the tall, good looking captain of the little collier *Endeavour* finally heard the words he had been waiting days to hear.

"Land ahead, sir," reported his young lieutenant.

The matter-of-factness with which Captain James Cook received this announcement belied the excitement he felt. The dark mass, hovering behind gray clouds of mist, became clearer. This strange land stretched as far as the eye could see. Smoke, curling up from several places, told the captain it must be inhabited. Green, rolling hills showed a gentle, forested land. Was this the new continent he sought? Was this Terra Australis Incognita?

Captain Cook ordered his helmsman to proceed northward along the eastern coast of the vast land. Surveying and charting as he sailed, the captain searched for a safe anchorage. But the waters were becoming increasingly difficult to navigate.

Unknowingly, Captain Cook was entering the treacherous Great Barrier Reef. This jagged coral wall paralleled the coast. And, to the north, it ran nearer and nearer the shore. The little *Endeavour* sailed on into a natural trap. As Captain Cook became aware of the trap, he sent out the longboats to precede the ship and take constant soundings. Navigation became a nerve-wracking nightmare, despite the skills of the captain. Then, with a shuddering, grating wrench, the *Endeavour* struck!

"Reef all sails!" ordered the captain at once. Longboats hurried to take new soundings all around the distressed ship. The collier, caught like a hooked fish on a knifelike outcropping of coral, beat violently against the reef. Great chunks of her hull and keel ripped free. As Captain Cook saw panic rising in his crew, he set each man to a hard, demanding task. His own calm manner reassured his officers and men. All turned to freeing the *Endeavour*. Stores were thrown overboard to lighten her. Pumps were started in her hold where the sea was flooding in.

For two days and nights, the captain encouraged his men at their exhausting, seemingly hopeless, labor. Finally the tide floated the torn and battered *Endeavour* free. Originally built to meet the rugged demands of carrying coal, this sturdy little collier had indeed been well chosen, thought her captain, as he maneuvered her on through the reef to shore.

While the *Endeavour* was being repaired, James Cook satisfied his deep curiosity about his new discovery. He explored the interior; gathered animal, plant, and soil specimens; and tried to make friends with the fierce, dark-skinned natives he often glimpsed in the distance.

Captain Cook had observed many different natives on the islands he had coasted during this voyage. His journals were full of notes he had taken on the ways and customs of both friendly and hostile tribes. The people of this strange Australis appeared to be the most primitive of all.

Whenever small bands of the natives were sighted, the captain hurried groups of his men toward them with gifts. But the savages, painted in thick red and white stripes, and brandishing poison-tipped lances, ignored the gifts and furiously chased the white men.

The *Endeavour's* crew became impatient. Why not show

these devils who was master here? "Let us turn our muskets on them," they pleaded. But Captain Cook respected the wish of these primitive people to defend their land. He forbade his men to fire upon the natives on punishment of death.

One day, in a stubborn attempt to convince the savages of his friendly intentions, Captain Cook ordered his men to stay behind. Alone, he walked toward a distant band of armed native warriors. The watching crew froze with fear for his life. As the captain moved slowly toward the savages, they raised their deadly lances. The captain did not falter. He continued slowly forward. As he reached a few feet from the dark-skinned men, he paused. The savages, without a sound, vanished like shadows into the forest.

The captain looked sadly after them and reluctantly returned to his relieved men.

Six weeks later the *Endeavour,* crudely repaired for the long voyage home, sailed back through the reef and headed for England. James Cook's mission had been successful. His four-year voyage of discovery, based on the old tales told by a few sailors of a vast continent "westward," opened up the unknown Pacific.

Few men were as well equipped to enter the unknown—and to survive its perils—as James Cook. Born in Yorkshire on October 27, 1728 young James had gone to sea on a merchantman at the age of eighteen. From the beginning, the captains under whom he had served, had known that this grave-mannered lad with the piercing brown eyes, was destined for a brilliant future. In the Royal Navy, James Cook rose to the rank of master, a term signifying the highest skills in surveying, navigation, and leadership.

His concern and care for his crews were legendary. Any eighteenth-century captain expected to lose at least half his crew to the dread scurvy on any voyage. Lack of fresh provisions and filthy quarters bred the fever. James Cook stocked his galley with carrot marmalade, juice of wort, and mustard: all excellent tonics against scurvy. And although Cook was more humane than most of his fellow-skippers, he applied the lash to any sailor who did not take his daily dosage of the foul-tasting anti-scurvy tonics. Crew's quarters were scrubbed well and often with vinegar, which served as a disinfectant. Extra clothes were issued to keep his crews warm and dry. Sailors on Cook's ships had a "good berth"!

The captain returned again and again to the Pacific after the Endeavour's voyage. He discovered the Hawaiian Islands, explored the western coast of North America, and mapped the vast, uncharted waters of the Pacific Ocean.

Captain James Cook was one of England's most outstanding explorers. He was highly respected as master-mariner and scientist. And his unselfish treatment of those who served under him won their undying affection and respect.

WILLIAM HALSEY, JR.

"Attack! Repeat, Attack!"

Admiral William Frederick Halsey, Jr. stood quietly on the bridge of his flagship, the U.S.S. *Enterprise*. On the flight deck below, his pilots waited for the take-off signal.

The big clock on the bridge read 4:43 a.m. Admiral Halsey gave the command to his air officer.

"All right, let 'em go!"

One by one, the planes streaked from the deck of the big aircraft carrier. Flying high over the blue waters of the Pacific Ocean, they headed for their target: the Marshall Islands. Halsey's men were on their way to give the enemy a dose of its own medicine.

On Sunday, December 7, 1941 American ships and planes based at Pearl Harbor on Oahu Island, had been attacked, without warning, by Japanese ships and planes. Within a few hours the whole world had known of the surprise attack. Japan and the United States were at war!

Now, two months later, on February 1, 1942 Admiral

Halsey launched his planes to strike the Japanese in the Marshall Islands. For ten hours, he held his small force of fighting ships in the dangerous Japanese waters. Enemy submarines, torpedo boats, and mines were in these waters. Twenty-one times Halsey's planes left the *Enterprise* to bomb and strafe the islands. The enemy lost many important shore guns and military supplies as well as thirty-five planes and eleven ships.

Finally the admiral called his planes back to their home carrier.

"Let's get out of here," he grinned. And as quietly and swiftly as he had brought them in, he led his forces out of the danger area, back to Oahu, victory flags flying!

The Marshall Islands raid was small compared to battles yet to come. But it gave new hope to the people at home. And it told the fighting men of the Pacific that they had a tough, brave leader in Admiral "Bull" Halsey.

Admiral Halsey was given the Distinguished Service Medal for this battle action. The night he received his award, he went down to the crew's compartments of the *Enterprise.* His men jumped smartly to attention when he came in. But he told them to sit down.

"I want to make a little speech," he said. And his next words made every man there feel honored to serve under his command. "I just want to say that I've never been so proud of anyone as I am of you!" As he walked quickly from the room, the cheers of his men roared through the ship!

The admiral was to command many more ships before the war ended, but his favorite was always the *Enterprise.* Her crew fondly called her the "Big E." This valiant carrier was in eight major battles in her first year of the war. Although the "Big E" took many hits, she kept fighting! She was the first ship of the war to be hit by a Japanese suicide plane—its pilot one of the Kamikazes, fliers who turned themselves into "human bombs" as they deliberately dived into American ships. The Japanese radio hopefully reported the *Enterprise* sunk so many times that the Americans happily named her "The Galloping Ghost of Oahu Coast"!

Admiral Halsey left the "Big E" to take over the fast, big battleship *New Jersey.* From her decks his battle cry of

"ATTACK, repeat, ATTACK!" was soon to be heard across the whole Pacific.

The Japanese had been secretly preparing for war for many years. They had built a mighty fleet of powerful ships. Halsey's forces were too small to stand and slug it out. And the enemy was swooping across the Pacific, gobbling up every island base in sight. Halsey had to work out some way to stop the enemy, to take them off guard!

He hit hard—and fast—and often! He tracked down the Japanese, charged in like an angry bull, and poured on everything he had! Then, before the surprised enemy could catch its breath, Halsey was gone!

In November, 1942 Halsey sent his fleet into the waters around Guadalcanal. The enemy wanted desperately to keep the island. U.S. Marines had landed and were trying to hold *their* position against day and night enemy attacks. The fighting was savage!

The Marines were suffering from battle fatigue and malaria. Their ammunition, medicine, and food were low. The enemy kept attacking day after day and night after night. The outnumbered Marines kept fighting back stubbornly, but the odds were great and they needed help. And then the news came that the "Old Man," Admiral Bill Halsey,

was sending help! The weary Marines took heart!

The violent battle lasted for five days! Both sides suffered heavy losses. But on the fifth day, Admiral Halsey could finally signal "Victory!" for the American forces.

"Well done!" he proudly told his weary men.

After almost three years of war, Japan showed the effects of Halsey's hard blows. The "Tokyo Express," which was Halsey's nickname for the Japanese fleet, had lost many ships and planes. And Japan did not have the manpower or materials to build new ones. The tide of war had turned! She must now try to defend herself!

Halsey *kept* battering the enemy with everything he had—all over the islands of the Pacific.

But despite Japan's losses, the greatest naval battle of the war was yet to be fought! American forces were to invade Leyte in the Philippine Islands. The biggest fleet ever seen on the high seas made ready to attack. Over seven hundred vessels—troopships, battlewagons, PT boats, cruisers, destroyers, and rocket ships—all awaited the signal.

First, Admiral Halsey's famous Third Fleet went to work, softening up the island's enemy forces. Then the soldiers hit the beach! Troops and tanks pushed their way ashore while planes fought overhead and ships stood guard at sea. The invasion had begun!

Suddenly scout planes and submarines reported that the whole Japanese fleet was speeding toward Leyte. This was to be the showdown! Admiral Halsey's Third Fleet, with Admiral Kinkaid's Seventh Fleet, moved out to meet the enemy.

For six thunderous days and nights, the seas around Leyte trembled under the deafening roar of battle!

When the smoke cleared, the end of the war was near. What little was left of the badly crippled Japanese fleet limped home.

The United States and her allies continued to beat back

the enemy, and within a few months, Halsey's fleet had fought its way to the very shores of Japan. On August 29, 1945 he led his ships into Tokyo Bay. Japan was ready to surrender!

The war was won! The job was done, and Bill Halsey was tired. He announced his retirement from the U.S. Navy.

"Let the young fellows take over," he said.

His hometown, Elizabeth, New Jersey, gave him a hero's welcome. Admiral William Halsey, Jr. had brought his valiant Third Fleet through the biggest, toughest naval war the world had ever seen.

Born on October 30, 1882 Bill Halsey grew up with the dream of some day joining the United States Navy. But he never dreamed that he would become one of her greatest admirals.

When he was given the honors paid to a returning hero, his words were again for the men he had led: "The finest fighting men of the world whom I have been privileged to command. I cannot say enough for them!"

JOHN PAUL JONES

Against All Odds

It was September of 1779.

Aboard the creaking, old *Bonhomme Richard,* a slight, swarthy man gazed leeward at the approaching British convoy. Forty-one unsuspecting merchantmen, each bulging with supplies for the enemy, sailed slowly into the American's trap. These supply ships would make rich prizes. But the eyes of the *Bonhomme Richard's* Captain John Paul Jones were fixed on the convoy's naval escort. Two warships, the trim, newly built *Serapis* of fifty guns, and the smaller but equally trim *Countess of Scarborough* of twenty-two guns, guarded the convoy. *These* were his targets, Captain Jones decided—and instantly bore down on them!

Suddenly the merchantmen sighted the American. Their guns cried out signals of distress. The *Countess* and the *Serapis* hurried to stand between their convoy and the rapidly approaching *Bonhomme Richard.*

Jones knew that this battle off Flamborough Head, on

the craggy east coast of England, would be the hardest he had ever fought. And he had fought many battles in his years at sea. Born in 1747 in the little parish of Kirkbean, Scotland, John Paul came from a decent, hard-working, but very poor, family. At twelve he left school to become a cabin boy aboard a trading vessel. A year later he made his first trip to America. This brave, new land at once captured the boy's heart. As a young man John was among the first to volunteer to serve in her War of Independence against England. He enlisted in the newly organized Continental Navy.

But his humble and foreign birth set him apart from his fellow officers who were wealthy aristocrats. Although Jones sank or captured more enemy ships than any other American, his rank remained among the lowest; his ships were never the best.

The old *Bonhomme Richard* was the poorest ship he had ever commanded! After an official mission to France, he found himself stranded there, without a ship to command, for over a year. Finally, in desperation, he bought a retired, old tub: the French merchantman, *Duras*. Captain Jones rebuilt her and renamed her in honor of a book written by his good friend, Benjamin Franklin. She became the *Bonhomme Richard,* "Brother Richard." Rusty old guns borrowed from a French arsenal made up her armament. Slow and balky, she was still little better than an old tub!

As the *Richard* sailed into battle with the *Serapis,* Jones checked the positions of his two escort ships. Standing off at a safe distance was the little French warship *Vengeance.* Riding far out to sea was the *Alliance,* a powerful, newly built French frigate. France had only recently joined America in the war against England. But the *Alliance's* captain, Pierre Landais, was one of those aristocratic officers who openly resented the success of this "American upstart," John Paul Jones. Jones could only hope that the jealous Frenchman would come to the aid of the *Richard,* if and when she needed it!

A bright moon rose as the *Serapis* and the *Richard* closed. Every man aboard the *Richard* knew that the British ship was greatly superior in size, speed, guns, and number of

men! As the two ships came abreast, Captain Jones gave the signal to attack. The *Richard's* guns thundered out the first broadside. Almost instantly an answering blast came from the *Serapis.* Jones's advantage lasted less than a second. In firing her very first broadside, two of the *Richard's* rusty, old eighteen-pound guns exploded, killing and wounding their gun crews and gutting the lower deck. The remaining four eighteen-pounders were worthless—too dangerous to fire. Before the battle was even properly begun, the *Richard* was afire, and minus her biggest guns!

The old ship was trapped! She could never have outsailed the enemy. Now she had not even a chance of outgunning them. Continued broadsides from the *Serapis* raked her side. The nearby *Countess* moved in, hurling broadsides at the *Richard's* stern. Jones prayed that the *Vengeance* or *Alliance* would move in to challenge the *Countess;* but the two French vessels, still at a safe distance, merely watched the struggle.

Then the *Richard's* main battery of twelve-pounders was gone—blasted to bits by enemy fire. Her hull, torn by the *Serapis'* big guns, was leaking badly. She was almost impossible to steer. Much more bombardment from the enemy and she would surely sink!

In Jones's mind a desperate plan began to form. With

incredible seamanship the captain maneuvered his crippled ship close in alongside the *Serapis*. Casting grappling hooks into the enemy's rigging, Jones's crew hurried to secure the two ships together. Jones himself rushed to make the *Serapis* fast with even more line. And now the two ships were bound side by side, bow to stern and stern to bow, like two furious stags with horns locked in deadly combat.

"Well done, my brave lads," cried Jones over the battle's roar. "We've got her now!"

The *Richard's* crew crouched ready on deck. Armed with cutlasses, muskets, and grenades, they awaited their captain's signal to board the enemy vessel. But Jones, who saw at once that the Englishmen were ready and waiting for the boarding attack, held back the command.

British guns and American guns now stood muzzle to muzzle. Smoke from guns on one deck engulfed the opposite sailors. Cannon balls from the *Serapis'* lower deck eighteen-pounders sliced into one side of the *Richard's* hull and out the other into the sea. Her side began to buckle! The *Countess'* guns were turned away. She was now engaged in a savage exchange with the *Vengeance* which had finally come into battle.

A new threat loomed to the *Richard's* free side. The *Alliance,* which had remained thus far safely out to sea, quietly moved in alongside the battered ship. As she crossed the bow of the *Richard* and the stern of the *Serapis,* a full broadside blazed from her lower deck guns.

Screams of horror froze in the throats of the *Richard's* crew. "The *Alliance!* The *Alliance* is firing upon us!"

In the bright moonlight the *Richard* was clearly recognizable to her French ally—but again the *Alliance* raked the locked ships with grape and cannister shot.

The nightmare battle raged on! By all the rules of naval warfare, the *Richard* should long since have gone to the bottom of the sea. Fire had broken out all over the ship. Water rose dangerously high in the torn hull. Enemy guns pounded her to splinters. And the *Alliance* readied for an-

other run. Panic swept the *Richard!* One of Jones's officers, half-crazed by confusion and fear, thought he was the last officer left alive on the ship. He called a surrender to the *Serapis!*

"Quarter!" he cried. "We call for quarter!"

"Do you ask for *quarter,* Captain?" roared back the *Serapis'* Captain Pearson in surprise. He could not believe that Jones would *ever* surrender!

Again came the disbelieving, but hopeful cry from the English ship. "Do you strike? Do you ask for quarter, Captain?"

Then Jones's answer rang out clear and calm above the clamor of guns and men.

"No, sir!" cried John Paul Jones. "No, sir! I have not yet *begun* to fight!"

The *Richard* was close to death. A sudden splintering crash came from the *Serapis* as her mainmast fell. At the same moment one of Jones's sharpshooters, perched high in the *Richard's* rigging, managed to cross to the *Serapis'* tops. He carried a basket of grenades and a lighted match. Swaying dangerously over the enemy's own deck, he dropped grenade after grenade onto the fighters and deck below. Explosions shook the warship as her magazines caught fire!

Again the call for quarter was heard. But this time it came from the *Serapis!*

The battle was over! As the smoke cleared, the two ships were cut apart. Battered and broken, they slowly turned toward France. But the price of victory was too great for the old *Bonhomme Richard*—two days later the valiant ship sank. Captain Jones and his men, aboard the *Serapis,* returned to France.

News soon spread all over the world of the incredible sea duel. But more important to John Paul Jones than his own glory, was the fact that this victory by an old French ship, captained by a poor, humble Scotsman, was won under the brave, young banner of the Stars and Stripes.

There seemed to be no excuse for the shameful actions of the *Alliance* except her captain's near-insane jealousy. When this was made known, the French Navy removed Captain Landais from his command.

For seven long and dangerous years, John Paul Jones fought for American freedom. At sea his daring tactics against a superior fleet helped to win colonial America her independence. His skill and knowledge helped to build her first navy. While he lived he received little recognition for his service to his adopted land.

But 168 years later, a much older, wiser, and more grateful country finally recognized his great contribution. In 1947 the Congress of the United States awarded John Paul Jones the Medal of Honor.

JACQUES-YVES COUSTEAU

Into the Depths

In 1936 Jacques-Yves Cousteau was a gunner in the French Navy. A powerful swimmer, he often spent hours in the sea, perfecting his style. One day a friend gave him a pair of underwater goggles. Curious, Cousteau put them on and peered down into the depths. A strange and startling new world greeted his eyes: delicately fashioned anemones in rainbow colors; sea creatures as small as a man's thumb and big as a man himself; graceful plants and seaweed dancing in sea-washed sunlight.

Cousteau knew that he must learn more about that mysterious underwater world.

As a skindiver, Cousteau made many dives using the traditional rubber fins and underwater goggles. But without a breathing apparatus, he could not stay under long enough to study the fabulous new world he had discovered. For eight years Cousteau experimented with breathing devices. An oxygen gear almost drowned him, as at that time it was

41

not known that pure oxygen under pressure would send a diver into convulsions. Again he narrowly escaped death when an air pipe from a surface pump broke.

Cousteau disliked air hoses and surface pumps. A diver, tied to a pump, was like a dog on a leash. A diver weighted down by a heavy suit and helmet was forced to crawl like a snail across the ocean floor. Cousteau wanted to keep the ease and speed that only skindivers knew.

With the help of an engineer, Cousteau finally designed a breathing apparatus which could be carried on his back. Air was fed automatically as needed. After several failures, the Aqualung was perfected. Now a "man-fish," with three metal cylinders of life-giving air harnessed to his back, was as free to move beneath the ocean's surface as *any* of its creatures!

Cousteau put the Aqualung to every conceivable test! As chief of his newly founded Undersea Research Group, Cousteau made underwater movies of sunken ships and treasures; he tested underwater explosives and their impact on divers. The group filmed submarine maneuvers and even tracked down a rare herd of white seals in an underwater cave.

One of Cousteau's most important *and* most dangerous problems was to study how the men-fish themselves reacted to the underwater world. Experimental depth dives taught Aqualung divers the terrors of the dreaded "raptures of the great depths." Great changes in pressure on the divers' bodies disturbed their nervous systems and made men, deep under the surface, go mad! Divers, suddenly feeling insanely joyous and powerful, could tear their mouthpieces from their mouths and drown, or they could black out at great depths—and never surface again.

Cousteau's group was asked to investigate an underwater cave near Avignon. No one knew how deep the cave ran. A guide rope, weighted by pig iron, was lowered ninety feet into the water. Cousteau and one of his best divers, Frederic Dumas, each wearing an Aqualung, rubber foot-fins, and carrying daggers and flashlights, were then lowered into the well-like cavern. A thirty-foot rope tied the two men together. The divers were to communicate with the surface crew by tugging on the guide rope. One tug meant "Pay out more rope, we're going deeper!" Six tugs meant "Emergency—haul us up in a hurry!"

As the two men descended, darkness enveloped them. Ninety feet down, Cousteau found the pig-iron weight. Shoving it off the ledge where it had caught, he watched it vanish into inky blackness. But his thoughts were hazy. His head began to ache as he followed the weight down, down, down. . . . His depth meter showed two hundred feet. Why was he here? Cousteau wondered. What was he to do in this strange place? Above him, a weird shape floated. He suddenly remembered Dumas. But Dumas, too, seemed curiously weak and confused. Dumas was blacking out! His mouthpiece suddenly slipped from his  slackened jaw, and before he could replace it, he swallowed water. Cousteau searched wildly for the pig iron. He must find the guide rope! This was their only way to safety, the only way to the surface.

Cousteau knew that he and Dumas were suffering the dread "raptures." But this had none of the insanely care-

free joyousness they had experienced in ocean-raptures. This was heavy fear, confusion.

Cousteau's flashlight beam flickered palely around the cavern. It caught the dim outline of the rusty metal weight. He grasped the guide rope and began to climb. He would climb the rope to the surface, pulling the unconscious Dumas up with him. But the diver suddenly realized that as he climbed, slowly, painfully, he was *not* moving *up*ward! Above, the surface crew had felt his first tug. The signal for more rope! Another tug, a pause, and another tug. Each time Cousteau grabbed the rope, more was lowered! Four hundred feet of rope passed through his hands. Now this *must* be the end! The crew above would surely pull them up. But a knot passed through Cousteau's hands. The unsuspecting crew above had tied on another length of rope!

Cousteau dropped the guide rope in despair. He must climb the sides of the steep cavern. He struggled up the

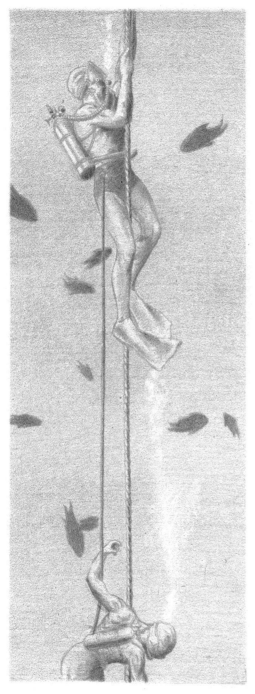

jagged crags, dragging himself upward, inches at a time. But as he reached for a higher hold, the dead weight of Dumas' body pulled him backward. He plummeted downward!

For a split second, his crazed mind told him that he must cut himself free of Dumas' body. Dumas must be dead, and he, Cousteau, was near the end. Reason struggled to break its way into his heavy confusion. A memory stirred dimly. The guide rope! The rope meant safety. If only he could remember what he was supposed to do with it! "Emergency. . . ." *This* was an emergency . . . and six . . . yes, *six* tugs would tell his surface crew!

Cousteau weakly grabbed the swaying guide rope. *Six tugs.* The rope grew taut in his hand. It began to move up! With the inert Dumas dangling limply, thirty feet below him, the exhausted diver was hauled rapidly to the surface.

When the two men had fully recovered, they decided, on a hunch, to run a lab test on the air in their cylinders. Horrified, the divers found that their lung compressors were defective—and were sucking back their own exhaust fumes! The Aqualung's exhaust, like the exhaust gases of a car, was poisonous if inhaled for any length of time. What Cousteau and Dumas had assumed to be their old enemy, the "raptures," was a new, and equally threatening, foe. A few more minutes would have meant death!

The valiant French diver-scientist has faced death many times in his long and colorful underwater career. But Jacques-Yves Cousteau continues to investigate the mysteries of the sea, a fearless and daring pioneer man-fish in an exciting new world.

DAVID FARRAGUT

"Full Speed Ahead!"

Rear Admiral David Farragut slept badly on the night of August 4, 1864. He arose before dawn, dressed, drank his hot tea, and sent his steward to check wind direction. Aboard the admiral's flagship, the man-of-war *Hartford,* Yankee sailors hurriedly downed coffee and sandwiches before reporting to battle stations. The battle for the Confederate stronghold at Mobile, Alabama, was about to begin.

For three years, civil war had divided the United States. David Farragut was a Southerner, born in the State of Tennessee. But he was also an officer of the United States Navy. The youngest midshipman in the history of the service, David Farragut had begun his career at the age of nine. When only twelve years old, he had served in the War of 1812. A lifetime on the seas of the world, in the service of the Navy, had earned him a reputation as a fearless, brilliant commander.

Now, in the war which pitted friend against friend,

brother against brother, David Farragut, the Southerner, was fighting in the Northern cause. Victory brought little joy to the slight, graying commander. But he must take Mobile. These were his orders.

Fort Morgan, which guarded the entrance to Mobile Bay, bristled with heavy artillery. To reach the city of Mobile, Farragut's Union fleet would have to run a deadly course past the fort, into the bay. The mouth of the bay was filled with piles, sunken hulks, and hundreds of newly invented explosive devices called torpedoes. Made of waterproofed kegs filled with gunpowder, these crude mines were held in place by heavy weights on the floor of the bay—and floated menacingly just under the surface. A narrow channel, marked by buoys, had been left clear by the Rebels for their own ships to pass. This narrow channel was the only path by which the Yankees might enter the bay.

The admiral checked last minute battle plans with his chief of staff. The iron-sheathed monitor *Tecumseh* would lead the way into the bay. Behind her, heading the battleships, would be the *Brooklyn*. Farragut's flagship, the *Hart-ford*, would follow the *Brooklyn*. The Union ships would enter the channel in pairs, lashed together by chain. If one ship were to become disabled, the sister ship at her side could tow her out of enemy cannon range. In the channel, barely wide enough to permit passage of the paired vessels, no Union ship must falter or she would foul the entire battle line.

At 7 a.m. the Union fleet moved slowly into the bay. Immediately the Rebel guns spoke. Farragut's ships thundered answering broadsides. Below the fort three Rebel wooden gunboats and the mighty Confederate monitor *Tennessee* opened fire. The Union's lead ships, *Brooklyn* and *Hartford*, drew devastating fire from the Rebel fort and ships. The *Hartford* was rocked from stem to stern—a blast from the *Tennessee* tore her mainmast in half.

Smoke rolled high, obscuring the admiral's view. He climbed hurriedly into the port main rigging. At once his

junior officers ordered the quartermaster to follow. Fearing
that their dauntless little admiral might be hurled into the
water, they insisted on lashing him safely to the rigging. Orders were relayed from his precarious perch as the flagship
continued to be raked by deadly fire.

Suddenly a rocking blast from off her bow shook the
Hartford. The Union monitor *Tecumseh* had forged past the
fort. The way had seemed to be safe. But then, with a terrible
roar, she hit one of the underwater mines. A great jet of
water exploded around her iron sides. Her bow slid under.
Her stern lifted high into the air. Behind the sinking
Tecumseh Farragut's lead ship, the *Brooklyn,* was now opposite the fort. Confused by the explosion, the *Brooklyn* suddenly stopped and backed engines.

From his station in the *Hartford's* rigging, Admiral Farragut watched with horror as his valiant monitor sank.

"Lower boats to pick up survivors!" he shouted over the battle's roar.

Confusion and panic swept the Union fleet. The *Brooklyn*, still backing, threatened collision for all the ships behind her. Completely out of control, she suddenly swung across the channel, blocking the battle line and narrowly missing the *Hartford*.

"What's wrong?" signaled Farragut to the *Brooklyn*. "Why have you stopped?"

"Torpedoes!" came the reply from the panic-stricken lead ship.

Farragut glanced quickly at his battle line of Union ships, now rapidly piling up—in danger of striking each other or of being forced to swing out of the safe lane between the buoys. Turning at once to the *Brooklyn*, he roared, "Damn the torpedoes! Full speed ahead!"

As the *Brooklyn* struggled helplessly to right herself, Farragut scrambled higher into the *Hartford's* rigging. Turning to his pilot, he suddenly called, "Is there enough depth for us to pass to the port of *Brooklyn?*"

The pilot nodded a puzzled affirmative—port side was torpedo side! But, trapped behind the *Brooklyn,* the Union ships were being pounded to splinters by the fort's heavy guns. Without a moment's hesitation, Farragut gave the order. The *Hartford* surged forward through the torpedo zone at full speed! The Union battle line, maneuvering around the *Brooklyn,* immediately raced after the *Hartford.*

As the Union ships streaked past the fort, no explosions sounded—not one ship went up in splinters of wood and iron. Farragut's daring strategy had worked! Counting on speed and the chance that at least some of the torpedoes would have become water-logged and harmless, he had led his fleet safely through the mine-infested waters.

Farragut anchored the *Hartford* four miles beyond the fort. As each of his battle-scarred vessels passed, saluting him with waving flag and cheering men, his heart filled with pride. When the Rebel *Tennessee* was sighted bearing down on the Union fleet, the Admiral's order rang out. "To all Union ships: attack the *Tennessee* with bows and guns at full speed!" After a violent skirmish, the *Tennessee* ran up the white flag. With her defeat, Fort Morgan surrendered.

Once again the Stars and Stripes flew over the city of Mobile.

Admiral Farragut was the hero of the hour upon his return East. Thousands welcomed him with cheers for "Daring Davy Farragut!"

Born in 1801, David Farragut spent sixty of his seventy years in the service of the United States Navy. The Navy's highest rank, that of admiral, was created especially for "Fighting Farragut." His loyalty to his men, his respect for knowledge, his steadfast devotion to the job at hand —as a young midshipman as well as when he became a respected admiral—keeps his name high on the list of the sea's great sailors.

JOSIAH CREESY

Best of the "Cracks"!

In April of 1851 crowds gathered at the Donald McKay Shipyards in Boston. Merchants and shipbuilders were on hand to witness the launching. All eyes were fixed on the new flag-decked clipper ship as she slid down the ways into the harbor. The largest merchantman afloat, the mighty ship weighed seventeen hundred tons. She carried a white and gold angel for a figurehead, and her name was the *Flying Cloud*. She was built for speed, the worthiest clipper ever built; and any clipper captain would have given all his worldly possessions to be named her skipper.

But her skipper had already been chosen. He awaited the *Cloud* in New York City. Seven weeks after her launching, the *Flying Cloud* arrived in New York Harbor to take on her cargo and her new master.

With Captain Josiah Creesy's first glimpse of the fabulous *Cloud,* he knew that his new command was the best of the "cracks." Clipper captains were a special breed among seamen. There was keen rivalry between clipper men. Sailing at speeds which, when compared to the pace of the old steamers, were hair-raising, the risks to ship and men were great. When storms raised great seas, the lightly built clippers were tossed like chips, sometimes staying on their beamends, or sides, for hours. The crews took on their captains' sense of rivalry. Sometimes, in important races, there was near-rioting when sail was reduced.

But despite the clipper crews' "racing fever," their seamanship was usually of the poorest quality. The gold fields of California beckoned landlubbers and sailors alike. Only the waterfront rabble was available to a captain looking for a crew. With a ship demanding incredible seamanship, yet manned by an incompetent crew, a clipper captain had to be a man of iron will and courage.

Josiah Creesy was such a man. Born in 1814 at Marblehead, Massachusetts, Josiah had been drawn to the sea from his earliest days. As a boy he sailed alone in a small dory all the way from Marblehead to Salem, just to gaze longingly at the Indiamen anchored there. These were ships which promised romance and adventure to a young boy. These were the ships which sailed to exotic, Far Eastern ports for spices, tea, and silks. Soon, Josiah had managed to get aboard one of the Indiamen, and was on his way to the Orient. By the age of twenty-three, he was himself a captain, sailing in the China trade. He soon earned a high reputation among the shipowners. He spared neither his men nor his ships in his runs. Captain Creesy became known as a "driver": the best of the clipper men.

And now he commanded the best of the clipper ships.

Captain Creesy sailed the *Flying Cloud* out of New York Harbor on June 2, 1851. Among his crew were men hoping for an easy passage to the gold fields, and men hoping for an easy way to fill their stomachs—even if they knew not the first thing about being sailors.

For the first few days the *Cloud* surged ahead on moderate west and northwest breezes, cutting smoothly through an easy sea. By the sixth of June Captain Creesy wrote in his log, "Good breezes, fine weather," as the wind rose and sent the *Cloud* literally flying across the sea. But the wind soon freshened to such an extent that, later in the day, the main and mizzen topgallant main were lost!

By the eighth, repairs had been made. The wind hauled around to south-southwest, and Captain Creesy ordered the main topsail yard sent up, and all possible sail set.

Creesy guessed that he was breaking all previous records set for the New York-San Francisco run. Similar "crack" clippers had averaged seventeen and a half knots—the *Cloud* was averaging twenty-one. Even the nonsailors in his crew marveled at the speed with which they sailed.

The weather held, but on the fourteenth Captain Creesy found that the mainmast was badly sprung, as a slender tree in a strong wind may splinter without fully breaking. He ordered repairs made, and with the mast strengthened, the voyage continued.

But the *Cloud* was soon to be put to the severest test of all. On the tenth of July she sailed right into a gale—a roaring inferno of blackness closed over her. Bearings could not be taken. The sun had vanished in a black sky. Violent winds raked the clipper! A mountainous head sea tossed her like a bucking bronco!

Captain Creesy was everywhere at once. The main masthead was sprung! The captain rushed his sailors high over the roiling seas into the rigging. Down came royal and topgallant yards. Off came the booms from the lower and

topsail yards. Men who had never sailed before snapped into action at their captain's rapier-sharp commands.

The *Cloud* sped forward at a ten-knot clip. Men went without food. They fell exhausted in their drenched clothes. The captain drove himself as he drove his men and ship! When the battered *Cloud* finally sailed out of the gale, the weary crew made repairs underway.

By August 25 the *Cloud* was off the coast of California. On the thirty-first, minus her fore topgallant mast, battered but whole, she sailed into San Francisco. In eighty-nine days and twenty-one hours, she had made it from New York to San Francisco. She was indeed a "crack" ship, declared her proud captain. Despite gales and an unskilled crew, the *Flying Cloud* had shattered all records!

For four years Captain Creesy continued to break all records with the *Cloud*. In 1854 he broke his own record on the San Francisco run—shortening it by thirteen hours!

In 1855 the captain, and Mrs. Creesy, who often accompanied him on his voyages, left the *Cloud* and went home to Salem for a rest. When the Civil War broke out, Josiah Creesy became a U.S. Navy Commander aboard the clipper *Ino*.

After his war service, he returned briefly to the China trade. But at the age of fifty-seven, he settled in Salem.

A short time later, the *Flying Cloud,* which had been sold to a British shipping company, caught fire and was destroyed. The era of a great skipper and an equally great ship had come and gone.

THOR HEYERDAHL

Six on a Raft

The strange wooden craft rode the sea like a bobbing cork. Waves as high as mountains rose up in front of her. They seemed ready to smash the frail craft to splinters! But lifted high on the crest of each thundering whitecap, the little *Kon-Tiki* plowed smoothly forward, pushing her way across the vast Pacific.

Under her open deck of balsa logs, the waters rumbled harmlessly past. In the center of the raft was a small, open cabin. Its walls and roof were of bamboo. Laid over the roof were tough, protective banana leaves. Over all billowed a big square sail. On its white canvas, painted in red, was the head of a bearded man. This was the head of "Kon-Tiki," ancient sun-king of the Inca Indians of Peru.

From the legend of Kon-Tiki came the raft's name— and its purpose. Her crew of six bearded, sun-browned young men were not making this dangerous four-thousand-mile sea voyage for adventure alone!

65

Thor Heyerdahl, a young Norwegian student and scientist, was the leader of the expedition. Years before, on a trip to the South Sea Islands in the mid-Pacific, he had heard a strange legend. These Polynesian island-people had told him of "Tiki," their ancient ancestor. It was Tiki—"chief," "god," and "son of the sun"—who had first come to these islands from a land "beyond the sea."

Thor puzzled over this legend. Scientists agreed that the Polynesians must have long ago sailed, or drifted, to these small coral islands. But from *where?* And *how* had they come? Thor thought he knew.

One of the legends of the Inca Indians of Peru, in South America, told of an ancient "chief-god, son of the sun." His name was also "Tiki"—but he was known to the Incas as "Kon-Tiki," which meant "sun-king." Warring tribes had forced Kon-Tiki to flee. Escaping with only a few survivors, he sailed westward, across the Pacific, never to return.

Thor had found other similarities between the Incas and the Polynesians. Their stone carvings, their customs, and even certain words in their two languages were alike! Were "Kon-Tiki" of the Incas and "Tiki" of the Polynesians one and the same? If so, how had Kon-Tiki reached the islands?

The ancient South Americans had no ships. But early Spanish explorers had written of the fishing rafts used by the Incas. Could these primitive, rough-hewn rafts of balsa logs have safely brought Kon-Tiki and his people over four thousand sea miles of Pacific Ocean? Thor believed they could and *had!*

66

"Impossible!" "Ridiculous!" replied Thor's fellow scientists when they heard his theory. The young Norwegian knew of only one way to prove it. He would build a raft like Kon-Tiki's. He would sail it over the same route: from the South American coast, westward, to the islands of the South Seas!

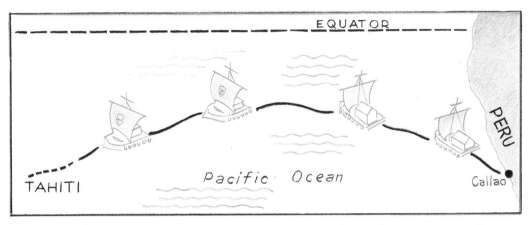

Months were spent in preparation for the voyage. Supplies, equipment, maps and charts, and crew were gathered together. Six men were needed to manage the raft, Thor decided. Herman Watzinger, an engineer, was the first to join the expedition. Three more were soon added. Knut Haugland, Torstein Raaby, and Erik Hesselberg eagerly replied "Yes!" to Thor's telegram invitation of "Am going to cross Pacific on a wooden raft. . . . Will you come. . . ?" The sixth member was Bengt Danielsson, an anthropologist. None of these men were expert seamen. But each brought a technical or scientific skill to the expedition. And Thor knew each man to be blessed, equally, with courage, even temper, and a sense of humor.

Now Thor turned to the building of *Kon-Tiki,* as the raft had already come to be known. Only in western South America could the proper balsa timbers be found. More months passed as the huge logs were located, cut, and floated down-river to the Pacific coast. At the Peruvian naval yards at Callao Bay the primitive wooden raft was built.

April 28, 1947 was the day of departure!

During their first week at sea, Thor and his crew felt  like infants at the controls of a spaceship! The combination of strong trade winds and currents battered the raft with high, choppy seas. The nineteen-foot steering oar behaved like a bucking bronco —two men could barely hold it in the boiling sea. Although it became clear that *Kon-Tiki* would stay afloat, she seemed intent on sailing with her stern as her prow. After three torturous days the weary men tied themselves into the little cabin and, hoping for the best, fell into a deep sleep. When they awakened, *Kon-Tiki* had righted herself; the seas had calmed. A bright sun bathed their ocean world in clear, bright colors. Erik checked the course. They were sailing westward, "into the sun," as the Incas' "Kon-Tiki" had, fifteen hundred years before them.

68

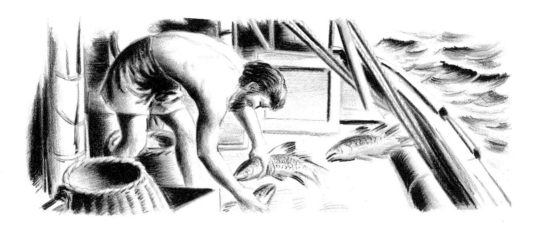

The men settled down to a strange, exciting new way of life. Curious visitors came to call! Flying fish flew onto the deck—sometimes men and fish collided with a loud, wet smack. But such annoyances were quickly forgotten when these tasty "flying missiles" wound up in a frying pan over the little primus stove. Many kinds of fish rounded out the crew's menu of coconuts, bananas, sweet potatoes, and army rations. And to quench their thirst, 275 gallons of sweet spring water were stored in cans, amidships.

Sometimes in the black nights, two mysterious, shining eyes suddenly rose up from the water and stared, unblinking, at the men. Perhaps, the crew guessed, these belonged to big squid, perhaps to huge fish from the ocean depths. Often below the raft, shimmering creatures, even larger than elephants, were seen. Since they never surfaced for air, they could not be whales. Were they giant rays? The men wondered.

One balmy May day Knut was washing his laundry astern. "Shark!" His sudden wild shout brought the others running. They stared.

Sharks were frequent visitors around the raft. But *this* was no ordinary shark! Grinning curiously at the startled

men, with his nose nuzzling the steering oar, was the biggest, ugliest monster they had ever seen! Its frog-shaped head had a jaw which measured four to five feet across. Long fringes, like moustaches, drooped from its mouth. Two tiny eyes gleamed wickedly in the sides of its head.

The monster swam lazily around the raft. Suddenly it dived *under* the raft! It was so enormous that its head jutted up on one side, and its tail flipped up on the other! This rare speciman was a whale shark. The largest fish in the world, it grows to more than fifty feet in length and may weigh fifteen tons! The expedition was not sorry to see its monster suddenly dash off and disappear.

Smaller sharks were an ever-present danger. But the

high-spirited crew invented a game which they called "pulling sharks' tails." A passing shark was lured to the raft's side by a dangling chunk of dolphin bait. As the shark snatched the bait, the crew grabbed the shark. If they succeeded in holding onto the wildly thrashing tail, they pulled him aboard for bait— or dinner. The record score: nine sharks' tails in one day!

There came a day when Thor thought the game had been reversed. As he knelt at a chore, aft, he was suddenly butted from behind by something very heavy and very wet. Without a backward glance, he flew up the mast. He was convinced that a shark had fastened onto his backside! When the crew finally stopped laughing, Thor learned that his "shark" was a three-hundred-pound tunny, crazily trying to leap aboard!

One great fear shared by the crew was that one of the

men might fall overboard and be left behind. Early in the voyage they learned that *Kon-Tiki* would sail valiantly forward. But she could not *stop*. Nor could she go *back!* In heavy seas, the men tied themselves to the raft to keep from being washed over the side. For if a man went overboard, he alone could save himself. And then it happened!

"Man overboard!" The men froze at the dreadful cry. Over the roar of the waves, they heard the faint call for "Help!" Far to the portside, Herman swam for his life. Knut and Erik grabbed a lifeline. By now Herman was astern, a few yards aft of the raft. He reached out to catch the end of the steering oar—it slipped from his grasp! A storm was moving in. Gusts of wind and an angry sea sped *Kon-Tiki* forward. Knut hurled the lifeline to the struggling swimmer. But, caught by the wind, it fell far short. Suddenly, from the stern, a figure dived into the sea. Knut was swimming toward Herman who was now hopelessly far behind the raft. In Knut's hand was the lifeline. High waves hid Knut, and then Herman, from their anxious comrades. But then came a fleeting glimpse of two heads, side by side, in the water. The men aboard hauled furiously on the lifeline. Knut and Herman were helped aboard, chilled and exhausted. There were still six men on the raft. But the *Kon-Tiki's* crew was singularly quiet and thoughtful that night.

Early one morning Herman, who was on watch, rushed into the cabin and roughly shook Thor awake. "Come out and have a look at your island!" he shouted with excitement.

Land! Far to the southeast it lay, a tiny, unmoving line on the horizon. *Kon-Tiki* had reached the South Sea Islands! But a strong current kept her far out to sea. Now she drifted toward the dangerous Takume reefs. Surrounding many of the mid-Pacific islands were underwater walls: reefs of coral. Ships caught in their treacherous currents and mountainous breakers, could be smashed to pieces. Now, like a

relentless slave driver, the wind drove the little raft toward Takume and disaster. The men quietly prepared for "shipwreck."

Ahead, peaceful little islands could be seen behind a wall of roiling surf. Cargo was lashed inside the cabin. The men put on their shoes for the first time in months. *Kon-Tiki* drifted closer and closer to the reef. Each man grabbed a guy rope and held on like a leech. Suddenly the raft lifted

high into the air. She was into it! As *Kon-Tiki* soared forward, riding the crest of a mountainous wave, Thor's feeling of unbearable excitement exploded.

"Hurrah!" he shouted, waving wildly to his friends. Before they could answer, the *Kon-Tiki* dropped—straight down! Tons of water crashed over the men who clung desperately to the ropes. Now *Kon-Tiki* was trapped. Waves twenty-five feet high hurled her skyward, then flung her furiously back to the sea. Wave after thunderous wave crashed over her, tearing at the men, deafening them!

A sudden blow jarred the raft. She had struck the reef! Again the men braced themselves as tons of water swept over them. But now the swell was lessening. The balsa logs surged up *onto* the reef. In a few terrible minutes *Kon-Tiki's* mast had snapped. Her sturdy cabin was now collapsed, her steering oar smashed. Safely beyond the surf, the men jumped out. They pulled *Kon-Tiki* into the quiet, shallow waters of the island's lagoon.

After 101 days at sea, her crew could again walk on solid ground. The bruised and weary men rested among the friendly Polynesians of these islands until a ship arrived to take them home.

Thor Heyerdahl did *not* prove that the ancient sun-god had made this forty-three-hundred-mile voyage fifteen hundred years before. But he and his brave crew *had* proved that such a voyage *could* have been made. *They* had made it!

EDWARD PREBLE

With Matches Blown!

The tall, redheaded commodore studied his log of junior officers. "What has the United States Navy come to," he exclaimed angrily, "sending a pack of boys to fight a war with treacherous, bloodthirsty pirates?" Commodore Edward Preble had been given the mighty U.S.S. *Constitution* 44 for his flagship. Six seaworthy craft rounded out his powerful little fleet. Each ship was manned by a stouthearted, well-trained crew. But the squadron of officers given him to command these ships and crews were "lads," he declared, "scarcely at the shaving age!" They were fine seamen and sea-fighters. But they were also hotheaded and reckless—fighting with each other if there were no enemy to battle!

Preble's "boys," in turn, had a few questions about their commodore. Born in Maine in the early 1760's, he could be as cold and silent as a Maine winter. His frosty gaze and ramrod bearing served as warning to the young men new to his command. Their high spirits and quick tempers had best be well hidden in the commodore's company!

Edward Preble's record of commanding men was a long one. He went to sea at the age of fifteen, aboard a merchantman. By the time he reached twenty-one, he was a United States Navy lieutenant with his own ship to command. A veteran of the American Revolution and the war with France, he was now bound for the Tripolitan War. Edward Preble was known as a battle-scarred, old sea dog. His "boys," by comparison, might be called brave, but foolhardy pups. This combination was to prove unbeatable!

In October of 1803 the *Constitution* sailed into the enemy waters of the Mediterranean Sea. Preble learned that an American ship had just been captured by the Emperor of Morocco. Its entire crew had been taken prisoner. Preble ordered Captain Bainbridge, commander of the *Constitution's* sister ship, the *Philadelphia,* to move on to Tripoli. He was to reinforce the blockade the Navy had already established there. The commodore himself would immediately call upon the emperor. A stop *must* be put to these outrages against American ships!

After the thirteen colonies won their independence, their trade vessels sailed out to new and distant ports. Some of their most important trade routes were in the Mediterranean. But ships sailing these waters were attacked by the Barbary Coast pirates! To prevent seizure of their ships, and imprisonment of their crews, some countries paid yearly "tribute" to the Barbary Coast states of Tripoli, Tunis, Morocco, and Algiers. For a while the United States, too, paid tribute money to keep her ships from being taken. In 1798 she "gave" the Bey of Tunis a quarter of a million dollars. But this only made the neighboring Bashaw of Tripoli, and the Dey of Algiers, greedily demand equal tribute. The United States then flatly refused to meet any further demands. The Bashaw of Tripoli promptly declared war on the unco-operative land across the sea. The other Barbary state pirate chiefs simply continued to take American ships —and to hold their crews for ransom. Since 1801 the little United States Navy had carried on a halfhearted war in the Mediterranean. In October, two years later, Edward Preble arrived with instructions from his government. He was to settle the matter, once and for all!

Preble now proceeded to Tangier, the capital of Morocco. He anchored his small fleet in the harbor, guns bristling and "matches blown," ready for action. Then, as he left the *Constitution,* he ordered that if he were detained ashore, the fleet was to blast the city to ruins!

Heavily armed, and accompanied only by two midshipmen, Preble went ashore. He demanded an audience with the emperor. When he was told that he must kneel before His Majesty, he refused.

"Americans kneel to no man!" Preble stated coolly.

He at once demanded the return of the American ship

and release of her crew. When the wily old emperor hinted that instead of releasing the Americans, he just might add Edward Preble to his collection, the commodore calmly invited him to look out the palace window toward the harbor. There the fleet waited, guns readied and aimed right at the palace walls. Not only was the emperor persuaded to free the Americans. He also promised not to seize any more American ships!

Preble and his men returned safely to the *Constitution.* But dreadful news awaited them! The *Philadelphia* was in enemy hands! In a chase with a Tripolitan corsair, she had run aground on an uncharted reef near Tripoli Harbor. Captain Bainbridge had tried desperately to free his ship. He had  braced his yards hard aback, cut away his anchors, cut away the foremast, and finally jettisoned his armament. But the heavy frigate was caught fast on the shoals. The ebbing tide hopelessly marooned her. Before surrendering, Captain Bainbridge flooded her magazines and chopped holes in her bottom so that the enemy could not salvage her. The captain and 315 men and officers were then taken prisoner by the Tripolitans.

But even worse was the news that, two days later, the *Philadelphia* had floated free. The Tripolitans had pulled up her guns, patched the holes in her bottom, and towed her into Tripoli Harbor. The Bashaw of Tripoli not only had American prisoners to hold for ransom! He had the mighty *Philadelphia,* which could be repaired and used against her own fleet!

A few nights after the *Philadelphia* was taken, Preble received a secret message from Captain Bainbridge. Written in lemon juice, the message had been smuggled from the Tripoli prison with the aid of a friendly consul. Bainbridge had a plan for destroying the *Philadelphia* in the harbor.

Among Preble's boys was Stephen Decatur, a fiery, young lieutenant. He begged to be allowed to undertake the dangerous mission in his own ship, the *Enterprise*. Preble preferred to use a small Tripolitan ketch which had been captured by the fleet. As a native ship, the little ketch had a better chance of getting into the harbor without arousing suspicion. Preble's plan was to send seventy-four volunteers, led by Decatur, to board the *Philadelphia* under cover of night and set her afire.

On February 7, 1804 the little ketch, now named the *Intrepid,* rounded for Tripoli Harbor. A sudden gale drove her back out to sea. For several days she ran high seas while rations spoiled or gave out and her crew went hungry. On February 16, the weather cleared. That night the *Intrepid* sailed quietly into the harbor. The readied volunteers were hidden down in the filthy, airless hold. Only a few men, disguised in native clothes, showed above deck. Decatur's pilot, speaking in the local tongue, hailed the *Philadelphia!*

"We carry supplies for the city," he called to her sleepy guards. His anchors had been lost in the storm, he explained. Might he tie onto the *Philadelphia* for the night?

"Permission granted," mumbled the unsuspecting Tripolitans. The *Intrepid* moved alongside. A rope was taken aboard.

"Americanos!" the alarm rang out. A Tripolitan sailor had seen the Americans crouching on the *Intrepid's* deck!

In a flash, Americans were up and over the side of the *Philadelphia*. With drawn cutlasses and pistols, Preble's boys cleared the decks! The confused Tripolitans who didn't jump overboard, were cut down instantly. Explosives were hurried below decks and set afire. Within seconds the *Philadelphia* was an inferno. Flames shot high. As the Americans tumbled over her side, down to the ketch, the surrounding Tripolitan ships suddenly came alive! The little ketch was silhouetted by the *Philadelphia's* fire. In the red glow now filling the harbor, she was a perfect target for the big shore batteries. Rowing feverishly, the Americans raced out of gun range, and out of the harbor to safety! Not one American was lost in the daring raid! Preble's boys were becoming men.

Their determined commodore maintained the blockade on Tripoli throughout the long, cold winter. The following summer he waged all-out war on the city. In daring surprise attacks, he brought the *Constitution* right into the harbor

to batter the shore defenses. Often Americans, fighting Tripolitan pirates in hand-to-hand combat, were outnumbered two to one! After five devastating raids, the city surrendered.

Reinforcements arrived from the United States, and with them a new commander for the Mediterranean area. Preble had broken the back of the pirate threat. He was to return home for a rest and new duties.

As the commodore said his farewells to his squadron, young Decatur stepped forward. He saluted smartly and presented a scroll.

It was signed by every one of Preble's boys: William Bainbridge, Stephen Decatur, Jacob Jones, Isaac Hull, David Porter, Isaac Chauncey, and many others whose names were to become immortal as fighting men of the sea.

The scroll read, "We, the undersigned officers of the squadron under your command, cannot allow you to depart without giving you some small testimony of the very high esteem in which we hold you as an officer and a commander." Edward Preble had won the hearts of his men as well as the gratitude of his young country.

GEORGE BRAITHWAITE

The High Gray Wall

Heavy, gray fog lay over *Nantucket Lightship 117* like a thick blanket. The *Nantucket,* like a sea-borne lighthouse, rode anchor a hundred miles off New England's rock-bound coast. No stationary lighthouse could be built on these surrounding shoals and reefs. No unmanned lightbuoy could yet be counted reliable enough to warn away approaching ships. *Nantucket Lightship 117,* with her mighty beacon, was sole guardian against disaster in these treacherous waters.

On the morning of May 15, 1934 the sea was quiet. There was little wind. Every fifteen seconds the diaphone, the fog horn, gave an earsplitting hoot. Astern, the submarine warning bell clanged monotonously. Four long notes from the radio beacon sounded over and over. As if the lightship were enclosed by a high, gray wall, there was no sound anywhere except these warning signals from the ship itself.

Captain George Braithwaite and his crew went about their daily routine. All moved quietly about their chores,

87

waiting for the fog to lift. But on deck, as if borne in on the soft, gray clouds of mist, lay an air of waiting, listening.

Suddenly Captain Braithwaite went forward. He leaned against the rail. His eyes probed the surrounding grayness. Standing motionless, his head cocked slightly to one side, he listened. Behind him the crew paused, listening too.

A low rumble like distant thunder rolled in on the fog. A minute later the sound was heard again—louder, closer.

"A steamer," thought the captain. "And a big one from the sound of that whistle!"

"Somewhere off the port bow," he called to his men.

The whistle continued at minute intervals. The steamer was approaching. The deck hands joined Captain Braithwaite at the rail. All peered anxiously into the milky grayness off the port bow. Fog was treacherous to any ship at sea. But to a lightship, it *could* mean death!

On this very morning *Lightship 117* had already been side-swiped by two fog-blinded vessels. Ships leaving European ports sailed in a straight line across the Atlantic Ocean.

The line began at their port of departure and ended at *Lightship 117,* the first beacon of light in American waters. Since 1854 ships had steered as straight for that beacon as a moth to a candle flame.

In clear weather an approaching ship could easily sight and run clear of the lightship's flashing beacon. But in fog Captain Braithwaite, an old-timer in the Lightship Service, knew strange things could happen to *sound* warnings. The heavy-set, sixty-nine-year-old New Englander had lived on or near the sea most of his life. Fog was the seaman's enemy —and on days like this, mused the captain, the vessels his lightship served were even worse enemies.

Now, as the captain and his men strained toward the sound of the oncoming ship, they heard nothing but silence. Even the muted cry of the whistle seemed to have vanished. The tension on *117's* deck rose even higher. Captain Braithwaite remained at the rail, motionless. Minutes passed. Suddenly the whistle's rumble again split the banks of fog. But now the sound was much nearer. Again it came at minute intervals; each time it seemed closer. Between the blast of the lightship's diaphone and the sound of the steamer's whistle, came quick pauses of heavy silence. A new sound broke the brief quiet: a sudden hissing. It came from off the lightship's bow.

"All hands on deck! On the double!" Captain Braithwaite snapped the terse order over his shoulder.

Sleepy men rushed from below to join their comrades at the rail. By now the hissing sound had increased to a loud and constant roar. But still nothing could be seen beyond that gray wall of fog!

The captain's hands suddenly gripped the rail. A gigantic shadow sliced through the gray wall before him. A shiny black hull as high as a six-story building loomed over *117's* bow. A whistle's muffled roar came from high above the heads of *117's* crew.

"Abandon ship, all hands— good luck!"

As *117's* men flung themselves seaward, their captain's sharp cry intermingled with the "full speed astern" gongs from the other ship.

But the signals came too late. From the forty-thousand-ton *Olympic's* deck, high over the lightship, Captain Binks looked down in horror. He shouted desperate commands. But the luxury liner continued to surge forward, slicing through *117* like a

knife through a loaf of bread.

The severed fore and aft sections of doomed *117* immediately disappeared into forty fathoms of bubbling, roiling, oil-slicked ocean. The surviving crew members and Captain Braithwaite, who was seriously injured, were quickly picked up by the *Olympic's* boats.

The mystery of why the *Olympic* struck its "target" so perfectly has never been solved. But the tragedy of *117* contributed greatly to the safety of today's lightships. The new *Nantucket 112* is practically unsinkable. New types of warning devices and alarms now protect lightships from oncoming, fog-blinded vessels. Interiors and exteriors have been redesigned to withstand collision. The ships have changed since *Lightship 117*. But the men remain the same.

Courageous, devoted men

like Captain Braithwaite are typical of lightship skippers. Other ships ride out or outrun storms; but the lightship, depending on her massive anchor, fights to stay at her station. She may be battered to the point of sinking, but the men of the Lightship Service know that no lightship ever leaves her station until a relief ship has replaced her.

This tradition serves as the end of the story of the greatest disaster in the Lightship Service.

Captain Braithwaite, in his hospital bed, knew that though *his* ship, *117,* was gone, a *Nantucket Lightship* was still at her station. Two days after the *Olympic* had sent *117* to the bottom, the luxury liner began her return voyage. The last beacon guiding her out of American waters came from a sturdy little ship with the name *Nantucket* painted in tall white letters on her fat red sides. Forty fathoms above the torn and twisted halves of *117,* rode *Nantucket Lightship 106,* standing guard against the treacherous shoals of the New England coast and keeping the light for all ships at sea.